ODE TO WE

ODE TO WE

RL RAHAMIM

illustrated by BETH RHODES

This work is dedicated to the hope of peace and reconciliation in all of our worlds, inside and out, but mostly in mine. ;)

It is dedicated to all of those who, in years of personal anxiety, have been strong to say "yes" and strong to say "no" or offer a listening ear. Mercy is the meadow I will remain captivated beside.

"Forgiveness is the sweetest thing..." –Isa Couvertier

CONTENTS

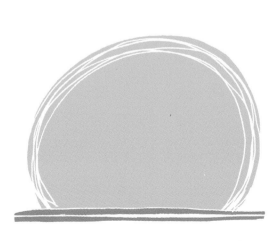

INTRODUCTION

Ode to We is an experiment, a practice, in negating the first or second person singular, and focusing on the first person plural, as a means of finding truth through various art forms and expressions, poetry included, of course! This is a means of eliminating lies by way of deduction and seeking truth in connection with the Other(s).

So, "we" is used, rarely "I" or "you", with some exceptions, since rules are just rules, and Mary Oliver said, "As long as you're dancing, you can break the rules/Sometimes breaking the rules is extending the rules."

I used this process in trying to forgive myself and not get down on myself so much. So, it started with this. It's a way of testing thoughts that can be intrusive.

Thought: I am a piece of shit.
First Test: Einstein is a piece of shit. (doesn't work)
Second Test: We are, as humanity, collectively, a piece of shit. (also doesn't work)
Connecting: I and Einstein are both humans/part of humanity.
Second Test Reflection: Humanity is most likely not a piece of shit.
First Test Reflection: I don't think Einstein is a piece of shit.
Therefore: I am, since I am part of humanity and so is Einstein, not a piece of shit.
Final Test: If "We are a piece of shit," sounds funny, then the thought is not true. :)
What has been proven?
Truth: Humans are not pieces of shit. *Lie:* I am a piece of shit.

Get it? These we statements bring us together and help us see ourselves more truly.

"Therefore the meaning of my life is not to be looked for merely in the sum total of my own achievements. It is seen only in the complete integration of my achievements and failures with the achievements and failures of my own generation, and society, and time...What I do is also done for them and with them and by them. What they do is done in me and by me and for me. But each one of us remains responsible for his own share in the life of the whole body. Charity cannot be what it is supposed to be as long as I do not see that my life represents my own allotment in the life of a whole supernatural organism to which I belong."

—From No Man Is An Island, by Thomas Merton

TIGHT TIN

inspired by listening to the audiobook Between the World and Me by Ta-Nehesi Coates
inspired by the timbre of Coates' voice and the meaning in Coates' words

It's the sound of our speech

Thumping

Against tight tin

It's the sound of our choices

Striking

Each raindrop

It's the sound of our echo

Ringing

For all to hear

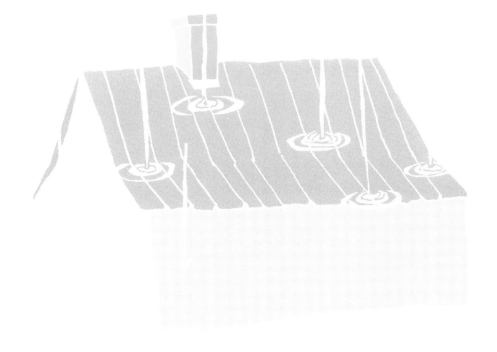

There's a sweetness that makes us get angry
It's a desire for the best thing to happen
We know what fun we could have,
We know how nice things could be,
We know it's possible for us to see
So, in order for the best thing to happen,
Can we move around just one or two things?

Enough,
And I'll
Use the
Water closet
So we
Can take
A break

Merciful more
Righteousness less
Has been the messy
Unbalance we've made
Not that any should be
Swayed for favoritism
May we be more "boring",
And by that I mean balanced
And matter-of-fact,
Like the bent water is "boring"
In this river

We didn't need music today as much
Waterfalls were occupying the emptiness
While Mary's words for Molly were whistling out
    faster than we knew they would
What a wonderful world
Where we can know Marys and Olivers
We do know them
We will need music to help them know us
When we can get the chance to express the inexpressible
Wisdom that is in our gratitude for their work

Nature You are our Mother Nature You are our sister more

We came out lonely from all the people

We will go back to them comforted with affection

From You

It's natural to need physical affection

It's logical that You would satisfy that necessity

We are not alone.

Do not be afraid.

The sun will rise

We will see another day

Wait

Nature is creating

A path in the wilderness

Where You are with us

Where love is limitless

We came out lonely from all the people

Nature You are our Ever Changing You are our affection more

Waving at those deer,
Away in the field,
While wearing
Red and green and green and red again
Shirt and sports bra and shorts and shoes

"Merry Christmas, deer!"

"Glad to see we're running
Together again
We'll be Santa Claus
And the reindeer,
But we won't bring anyone any things;
And we'll be free and
We'll call it all love"

We did the things today
We ate the food
We can be grateful
We can be good

CUSSING (CURSING)

For a long time we were
Too young to cuss (curse) publicly
Because we were not confident
Of our identity enough
To offend others with love
From lack of experience

She said,

"It's selfish,"

And I agree

Because it's

What is said

To the brokenly

To the lowly

To the lost

To the ugly

That needs

To be shared

We've all

We will all

Be there

So please

Help us

To have the time

To have the place

To have the help

To share

We, all of us,

If we dare

Life
happened
To us
It will
happen
Tomorrow
It is
happening
Now
Walk

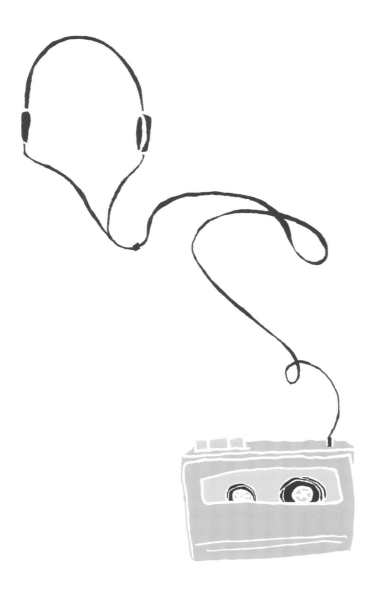

Feminist We

May be,

But

George Strait,

Cowboy hat and all,

Just gave us

A thumbs up

Toward the end

Of a long run

And it was Life

And we are Not The Same

The hill tops out

Past the hidden entrance

It's at the open, narrow, swinging, red gate

We leave it open,

Oh, and

It's narrow so you have to just walk through,

Okay…

Let's walk back down now

More awake

Less lonely for some reason

Oh!

Can we dance a little

On the long walk down?

Oh!

Can we listen

To Paul Simon sing,

"Why deny the obvious child?"?!

yes we'll add music
because it's moving
so we can be still

We were there once
Then we were here now
If it's okay with you
If it's okay with me
We'll all be free

To express

This reality

Is art

So an experiment

To speak

To write

To relay

Why or How it is

That we come

To feel

TOO TAME!

Too tame, everyone!
While we want to paint
WAIT
Onto our walls

We can be free

Put the lighter
Or the match
Beside the candle
So we don't forget
Where the light came from.

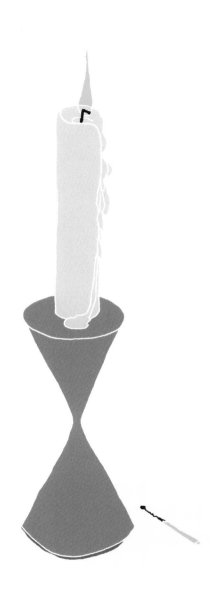

OKAY

Okay
Okay

Wisdom says,
"Start again,"
And we will
Be trusting
Will we ever
Be the same
We are everchanging
Our nearness
Of heart and
Of conversation
May be damaged
Or compromised
But we will fight
Being afraid
We will let love
Give flight
We will let go
Of the deadly way
Of life
Of the spinning mind
Of war...
That's something
Worth being
Sorry for...

We'll run while we can
Then we'll walk when we need to
Life seems to be good

A tree grows
And we are healed

The sun goes down over Dolly Parton bridge…

I guess it takes more than a song…

More than a king…

For such a fight…

Graceland is a ghost town tonight…

We sang together in the Lincoln theatre

It was all of us singing

Coming together in

A duet

That field belongs to our heart

Do they know?

We think they do

That's why they are taking such good care of it

Because they know we need it every now and then

To visit on lonely days when it's not sunny anywhere else

They are always keeping a little space for us

Kind of them to share a few spare sunsets

We look like the sea

We look like the sky

We look like that mountainside—deep,

We look like those trees,

With all of their rings,

You, looking at me

We look like the sky

We look like the sea

May we always be like those rivers

May we always be flowing

Free

Long live the undiscoverable vast of the sea!

Long live the waves washing over our feet.

Long live You

Long live We

WHEN WE MET
inspired by a brief meeting with Michael Kiwanuka,
after his performance at the Bottle Tree in Birmingham, AL

When we met

We met

And now we know

We know

BUZZING

So many bees buzzing by are our inspirations right now
And we may not catch them all,
For freedom belongs to you, too, God
We will go to sleep now
So you can be free?
After we write a little more down
—those bees buzzing through—
Let us just catch one more, or two,
Because the honey today is so good
And we want to stop them and say,
"Thank you, thank you,
See you tomorrow,
We'll miss you!"

I'm sorry for trying to possess you
We can do better than that
I'm sorry for trying to possess me
We are too much of a mystery
Even on our best days,
And the worst,
We are only made
In the likeness of Us.
Oh, please say, "We can start again,
friend."

We can hug

We can sit

We can eat

We can fear

We can love

We can listen

We can hush

We can smile

We can laugh

We can look

We can see

We can question

We can admit

We can speak

We can hear

We can need

We can ride

We can hydrate

We can notice

We can care

We can help

We can assure

We can come

We can go

We can visit

We can quiet

We can excuse

We can correct

We can encourage

We can discourage

We can agree

We can disagree

We can inside

We can outside

We can grow

We can shrink

We can dance

We can sing

We can borrow

We can lend

We can buy

We can sell

We can cover

We can uncover

We can more

We can less

Once again

Ode to We

Surprising
To see
How loving
We can be
Our living
So free
Relieving
Relief

MERCY

We were never told
Or we didn't hear
Learning to ask
As we grow old
Mercy for every mask
Calling itself bold
Behaving as ass
Cool mostly cold–
Heartedly crass

And I can say

For certain

No other

Can know

How it is

To be me

And you can say

For sure

None else

Can see

The way

To be you

And we can say

Forever

Yes

Once again

Let it be

Ode to we

All of us

We don't wanna come down
From this hill
Because it took us such time
And we're not sure
We can stand
Another incline

We are
So beautiful

And this one
And that one
And this way
And that way
And we will
And we have

SMALL BIRD

Why scared
To touch
Hold onto
That which
We could crush

What?

We took

Them with us

Didn't we?

Where were

We supposed to be?

How was I supposed to know?

No I didn't ask anyone.

Well I don't know why?

I'm sorry, but

Is it wrong to ask

If there will be

Another time?

Would it help

If we smiled?

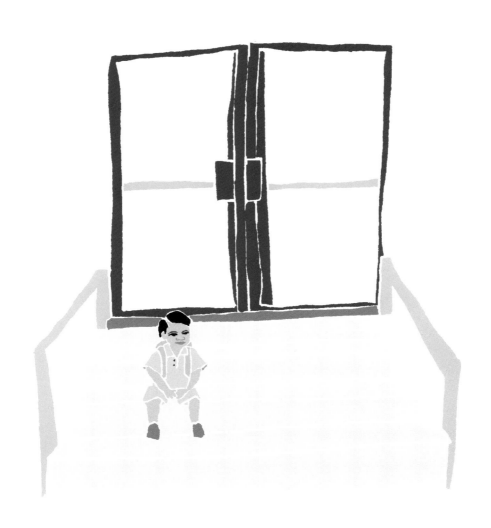

come

inside

from

without

and find us,

find us out

so one day

and today

we will

we are

we were

already

free.

Mostly…

Maybe

We are not

We are

What it seems

~~Who~~

How?

Maybe a map

Mostly love

WALKING BENEATH

Walking beneath

Widow makers

We will

Risk walking

One more

While

We is

seeing and

searching

for

each other

Where the weed was
It dried up in the sun
So let's lay down there
And remember rest

Why so hard
to trust love?
It seems to be
too good to be true?
And we have
so much

Competing

We

Fall

Down

We

Push

Down

Friendly

We

Fall

In

We

Push

Up

Through

the

Ground

Toward

The

Sky

Who are you?

Lily, who are you?

Honey, where did you come from?

Heaven…and Earth, where did you come from?

Here…and over there, where is Heaven?

Here…and Over There

Always how the ground is small
And I've found a place
We're small too, ground
We're tall too, trees
We're peaceful, river,
and flowing
Together
So many pieces
Bent
So water can move
Around winding Wheres
To take us to places
We're bent too, water
We're winding around where we can
We're so many small pieces
Making small people
Making small world
Making small space
Where we can
Be like each other
In our ways
Where we can
Otherwise we'll wind
There is time

LAY DOWN

Can we
lay down
with the lion,
lamb?

TRUE

We

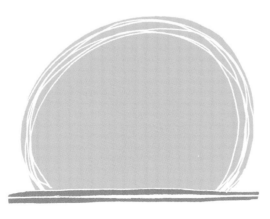

CPSIA information can be obtained at www.ICGtesting.com
Printed in the USA
LVIW01n2058160917
548924LV00003B/3